STATUTORY INSTRUMENTS

2003 No. 3096

LANDLORD AND TENANT, ENGLAND AND WALES

REGULATORY REFORM

Approved by both Houses of Parliament

The Regulatory Reform (Business Tenancies) (England and Wales) Order 2003

Made - - - - -	*1st December 2003*
Coming into force - -	*1st June 2004*

Whereas

(a) the First Secretary of State has consulted(**a**)—

    (i) such organisations as appear to him to be representative of interests substantially affected by his proposals for this Order,

    (ii) the National Assembly for Wales,

    (iii) the Law Commission, and

    (iv) such other persons as he considered appropriate;

(b) as a result of that consultation it appeared to the First Secretary of State that it was appropriate to vary part of his proposals, and he undertook such further consultation with respect to the variations as appeared to him appropriate;

(c) following the consultation mentioned in recitals (a) and (b) the First Secretary of State considered it appropriate to proceed with the making of this Order;

(d) a document containing the First Secretary of State's proposals was laid before Parliament as required by section 6 of the Regulatory Reform Act 2001(**b**) and the period for Parliamentary consideration under section 8 of that Act expired;

(e) the First Secretary of State had regard to the representations made during that period and, in particular, to the reports of the House of Commons Regulatory Reform Committee (Second Report, Session 2002–03, HC182) and the House of Lords Select Committee on Delegated Powers and Regulatory Reform (Fourth Report, Session 2002–03), HL Paper 22);

(f) a draft of this Order was laid before Parliament with a statement giving details of those representations and the changes to the First Secretary of State's proposals in the light of them;

(g) the draft was approved by a resolution of each of House of Parliament;

(**a**) By virtue of section 5(4) of the Regulatory Reform Act 2001 (c. 6), consultation undertaken before 10 April 2001 (the day on which that Act was passed) is treated as satisfying the consultation requirements of section 5(1) of that Act to the extent that, if it had been undertaken after that day, it would have satisfied those requirements. A consultation paper "Business tenancies legislation in England and Wales: the Government's proposals for reform" was published by the Department of the Environment, Transport and the Regions in March 2001. Copies may be obtained from Land and Property Division, Office of the Deputy Prime Minister, Eland House, Bressenden Place SW1E 5DU (tel: 020 7944 5559).

(**b**) 2001 c. 6.

[ODPM 2817]

(h) this Order modifies a function of the National Assembly for Wales and the Assembly has agreed that it be made;

(i) the First Secretary of State is of the opinion that this Order does not remove any necessary protection or prevent any person from continuing to exercise any right or freedom which he might reasonably expect to continue to exercise; and

(j) this Order creates burdens affecting persons in the carrying on of certain activities, and the First Secretary of State is of the opinion that—

(i) the provisions of this Order, taken as a whole, strike a fair balance between the public interest and the interests of the persons affected by the burdens being created, and

(ii) the extent to which this Order removes or reduces one or more burdens, or has other beneficial effects for persons affected by the burdens imposed by the existing law, makes it desirable for this Order to be made;

Now therefore the First Secretary of State, in exercise of the powers conferred by sections 1 and 4 of the Regulatory Reform Act 2001, hereby makes the following Order:—

Introduction

Citation, commencement and interpretation

1.—(1) This Order may be cited as the Regulatory Reform (Business Tenancies) (England and Wales) Order 2003.

(2) This Order extends to England and Wales only.

(3) This Order shall come into force at the end of the period of 6 months beginning with the day on which it is made.

(4) In this Order, "the Act" means the Landlord and Tenant Act 1954(**a**).

Amendment of the Landlord and Tenant Act 1954

2. The Act shall be amended as follows.

Applications to court by landlord or tenant

Amendments to section 24

3.—(1) In section 24(1)(**b**) (continuation of business tenancies), for the words "provisions of section twenty-nine of this Act, the tenant under such a tenancy may apply to the court for" substitute the words "following provisions of this Act either the tenant or the landlord under such a tenancy may apply to the court for an order for the grant of".

(2) Insert the following subsections after section 24(2)—

"(2A) Neither the tenant nor the landlord may make an application under subsection (1) above if the other has made such an application and the application has been served.

(2B) Neither the tenant nor the landlord may make such an application if the landlord has made an application under section 29(2) of this Act and the application has been served.

(2C) The landlord may not withdraw an application under subsection (1) above unless the tenant consents to its withdrawal.".

Amendments to section 25

4.—(1) Omit section 25(5) (requirement for tenant to notify landlord whether he is willing to give up possession).

(2) For section 25(6) substitute—

"(6) A notice under this section shall not have effect unless it states whether the landlord is opposed to the grant of a new tenancy to the tenant.

(**a**) 2 & 3 Eliz. 2 c. 56.

(**b**) Section 24(1) was amended by section 3(2) of the Law of Property Act 1969 (c. 59).

(7) A notice under this section which states that the landlord is opposed to the grant of a new tenancy to the tenant shall not have effect unless it also specifies one or more of the grounds specified in section 30(1) of this Act as the ground or grounds for his opposition.

(8) A notice under this section which states that the landlord is not opposed to the grant of a new tenancy to the tenant shall not have effect unless it sets out the landlord's proposals as to—

    (a) the property to be comprised in the new tenancy (being either the whole or part of the property comprised in the current tenancy);

    (b) the rent to be payable under the new tenancy; and

    (c) the other terms of the new tenancy.".

Landlord's application to terminate tenancy

5. For section 29 (order by court for grant of a new tenancy) and the cross-heading immediately preceding it substitute—

"Applications to court

Order by court for grant of new tenancy or termination of current tenancy

29.—(1) Subject to the provisions of this Act, on an application under section 24(1) of this Act, the court shall make an order for the grant of a new tenancy and accordingly for the termination of the current tenancy immediately before the commencement of the new tenancy.

(2) Subject to the following provisions of this Act, a landlord may apply to the court for an order for the termination of a tenancy to which this Part of this Act applies without the grant of a new tenancy—

    (a) if he has given notice under section 25 of this Act that he is opposed to the grant of a new tenancy to the tenant; or

    (b) if the tenant has made a request for a new tenancy in accordance with section 26 of this Act and the landlord has given notice under subsection (6) of that section.

(3) The landlord may not make an application under subsection (2) above if either the tenant or the landlord has made an application under section 24(1) of this Act.

(4) Subject to the provisions of this Act, where the landlord makes an application under subsection (2) above—

    (a) if he establishes, to the satisfaction of the court, any of the grounds on which he is entitled to make the application in accordance with section 30 of this Act, the court shall make an order for the termination of the current tenancy in accordance with section 64 of this Act without the grant of a new tenancy; and

    (b) if not, it shall make an order for the grant of a new tenancy and accordingly for the termination of the current tenancy immediately before the commencement of the new tenancy.

(5) The court shall dismiss an application by the landlord under section 24(1) of this Act if the tenant informs the court that he does not want a new tenancy.

(6) The landlord may not withdraw an application under subsection (2) above unless the tenant consents to its withdrawal.".

Amendments to section 30

6.—(1) In section 30(1) (grounds of opposition by landlord to renewal of tenancy), for the words "subsection (1) of section twenty-four of this Act" substitute "section 24(1) of this Act, or make an application under section 29(2) of this Act,".

(2) In section 30(2), after the words "oppose an application" insert "under section 24(1) of this Act, or make an application under section 29(2) of this Act,".

Amendment to section 31

7. In section 31(2) (declaration and order of the court in certain cases where landlord opposes renewal) for the words from the beginning to "any of those grounds" substitute "Where the landlord opposes an application under section 24(1) of this Act, or makes an application under section 29(2) of this Act, on one or more of the grounds specified in section 30(1)(d) to (f) of this Act but establishes none of those grounds, and none of the other grounds specified in section 30(1) of this Act, to the satisfaction of the court, then if the court would have been satisfied on any of the grounds specified in section 30(1)(d) to (f) of this Act".

Amendment to section 31A

8. In section 31A(1)(**a**) (grant of new tenancy in some cases where section 30(1)(f) applies), after the words "30(1) of this Act" insert ", or makes an application under section 29(2) of this Act on that ground,".

Amendment to section 34

9. In section 34(2)(a) (**b**) (rent under new tenancy), for the words "for the new tenancy" substitute the words "to the court".

Time limits for applications to court

10. After section 29 insert the following sections—

"Time limits for applications to court

29A.—(1) Subject to section 29B of this Act, the court shall not entertain an application—

    (a) by the tenant or the landlord under section 24(1) of this Act; or

    (b) by the landlord under section 29(2) of this Act,

    if it is made after the end of the statutory period.

(2) In this section and section 29B of this Act "the statutory period" means a period ending—

    (a) where the landlord gave a notice under section 25 of this Act, on the date specified in his notice; and

    (b) where the tenant made a request for a new tenancy under section 26 of this Act, immediately before the date specified in his request.

(3) Where the tenant has made a request for a new tenancy under section 26 of this Act, the court shall not entertain an application under section 24(1) of this Act which is made before the end of the period of two months beginning with the date of the making of the request, unless the application is made after the landlord has given a notice under section 26(6) of this Act.

Agreements extending time limits

29B.—(1) After the landlord has given a notice under section 25 of this Act, or the tenant has made a request under section 26 of this Act, but before the end of the statutory period, the landlord and tenant may agree that an application such as is mentioned in section 29A(1) of this Act, may be made before the end of a period specified in the agreement which will expire after the end of the statutory period.

(2) The landlord and tenant may from time to time by agreement further extend the period for making such an application, but any such agreement must be made before the end of the period specified in the current agreement.

(3) Where an agreement is made under this section, the court may entertain an application such as is mentioned in section 29A(1) of this Act if it is made before the end of the period specified in the agreement.

(**a**) Section 31A was inserted by section 7(1) of the Law of Property Act 1969 (c. 59).
(**b**) Section 34(2) was inserted by section 1(1) of the Law of Property Act 1969.

(4) Where an agreement is made under this section, or two or more agreements are made under this section, the landlord's notice under section 25 of this Act or tenant's request under section 26 of this Act shall be treated as terminating the tenancy at the end of the period specified in the agreement or, as the case may be, at the end of the period specified in the last of those agreements.".

Amendment to section 25

11. In section 25(1) (termination of tenancy subject to provisions of Part 4) after "subject to" insert "the provisions of section 29B(4) of this Act and".

Amendment to section 26

12. In section 26(5) (termination of tenancy subject to section 36(2) and Part 4) for "subsection (2) of section thirty-six" substitute "sections 29B(4) and 36(2)".

Companies and their controlling shareholders

Amendment to section 23

13. After section 23(1) (tenancies to which Part 2 applies) insert—

"(1A) Occupation or the carrying on of a business—

    (a) by a company in which the tenant has a controlling interest; or

    (b) where the tenant is a company, by a person with a controlling interest in the company,

shall be treated for the purposes of this section as equivalent to occupation or, as the case may be, the carrying on of a business by the tenant.

(1B) Accordingly references (however expressed) in this Part of this Act to the business of, or to use, occupation or enjoyment by, the tenant shall be construed as including references to the business of, or to use, occupation or enjoyment by, a company falling within subsection (1A)(a) above or a person falling within subsection (1A)(b) above.".

Amendments to section 30

14.—(1) After section 30(1) (opposition by landlord to renewal of tenancy) insert—

"(1A) Where the landlord has a controlling interest in a company, the reference in subsection (1)(g) above to the landlord shall be construed as a reference to the landlord or that company.

(1B) Subject to subsection (2A) below, where the landlord is a company and a person has a controlling interest in the company, the reference in subsection (1)(g) above to the landlord shall be construed as a reference to the landlord or that person."

(2) After section 30(2) insert—

"(2A) Subsection (1B) above shall not apply if the controlling interest was acquired after the beginning of the period of five years which ends with the termination of the current tenancy, and at all times since the acquisition of the controlling interest the holding has been comprised in a tenancy or successive tenancies of the description specified in section 23(1) of this Act.".

Amendment to section 34

15. After section 34(2) (improvements to which subsection (1)(c) applies) insert—

"(2A) If this Part of this Act applies by virtue of section 23(1A) of this Act, the reference in subsection (1)(d) above to the tenant shall be construed as including—

    (a) a company in which the tenant has a controlling interest, or

    (b) where the tenant is a company, a person with a controlling interest in the company.".

Amendment to section 42

16. At the end of the first paragraph of section 42(1)(**a**) (groups of companies) add "or the same person has a controlling interest in both".

Amendments to section 46

17.—(1) Section 46 (interpretation of Part 2) shall become section 46(1).

(2) After that subsection add—

"(2) For the purposes of this Part of this Act, a person has a controlling interest in a company, if, had he been a company, the other company would have been its subsidiary; and in this Part—

"company" has the meaning given by section 735 of the Companies Act 1985; and

"subsidiary" has the meaning given by section 736 of that Act.".

Interim rent

Rent while tenancy continues by virtue of section 24

18. For section 24A(**b**) (interim rent) substitute—

"Applications for determination of interim rent while tenancy continues

24A—(1) Subject to subsection (2) below, if—

(a) the landlord of a tenancy to which this Part of this Act applies has given notice under section 25 of this Act to terminate the tenancy; or

(b) the tenant of such a tenancy has made a request for a new tenancy in accordance with section 26 of this Act,

either of them may make an application to the court to determine a rent (an "interim rent") which the tenant is to pay while the tenancy ("the relevant tenancy") continues by virtue of section 24 of this Act and the court may order payment of an interim rent in accordance with section 24C or 24D of this Act.

(2) Neither the tenant nor the landlord may make an application under subsection (1) above if the other has made such an application and has not withdrawn it.

(3) No application shall be entertained under subsection (1) above if it is made more than six months after the termination of the relevant tenancy.

Date from which interim rent is payable

24B—(1) The interim rent determined on an application under section 24A(1) of this Act shall be payable from the appropriate date.

(2) If an application under section 24A(1) of this Act is made in a case where the landlord has given a notice under section 25 of this Act, the appropriate date is the earliest date of termination that could have been specified in the landlord's notice.

(3) If an application under section 24A(1) of this Act is made in a case where the tenant has made a request for a new tenancy under section 26 of this Act, the appropriate date is the earliest date that could have been specified in the tenant's request as the date from which the new tenancy is to begin.

Amount of interim rent where new tenancy of whole premises granted and landlord not opposed

24C—(1) This section applies where—

(a) the landlord gave a notice under section 25 of this Act at a time when the tenant was in occupation of the whole of the property comprised in the relevant tenancy for purposes such as are mentioned in section 23(1) of this Act and stated in the notice that he was not opposed to the grant of a new tenancy; or

---

(**a**) Section 42(1) was amended by paragraph 3 of Schedule 18 to the Companies Act 1989 (c. 40).

(**b**) Section 24A was inserted by section 4(1) of the Law of Property Act 1969.

6

(b) the tenant made a request for a new tenancy under section 26 of this Act at a time when he was in occupation of the whole of that property for such purposes and the landlord did not give notice under subsection (6) of that section,

and the landlord grants a new tenancy of the whole of the property comprised in the relevant tenancy to the tenant (whether as a result of an order for the grant of a new tenancy or otherwise).

(2) Subject to the following provisions of this section, the rent payable under and at the commencement of the new tenancy shall also be the interim rent.

(3) Subsection (2) above does not apply where—

(a) the landlord or the tenant shows to the satisfaction of the court that the interim rent under that subsection differs substantially from the relevant rent; or

(b) the landlord or the tenant shows to the satisfaction of the court that the terms of the new tenancy differ from the terms of the relevant tenancy to such an extent that the interim rent under that subsection is substantially different from the rent which (in default of such agreement) the court would have determined under section 34 of this Act to be payable under a tenancy which commenced on the same day as the new tenancy and whose other terms were the same as the relevant tenancy.

(4) In this section "the relevant rent" means the rent which (in default of agreement between the landlord and the tenant) the court would have determined under section 34 of this Act to be payable under the new tenancy if the new tenancy had commenced on the appropriate date (within the meaning of section 24B of this Act).

(5) The interim rent in a case where subsection (2) above does not apply by virtue only of subsection (3)(a) above is the relevant rent.

(6) The interim rent in a case where subsection (2) above does not apply by virtue only of subsection (3)(b) above, or by virtue of subsection (3)(a) and (b) above, is the rent which it is reasonable for the tenant to pay while the relevant tenancy continues by virtue of section 24 of this Act.

(7) In determining the interim rent under subsection (6) above the court shall have regard—

(a) to the rent payable under the terms of the relevant tenancy; and

(b) to the rent payable under any sub-tenancy of part of the property comprised in the relevant tenancy,

but otherwise subsections (1) and (2) of section 34 of this Act shall apply to the determination as they would apply to the determination of a rent under that section if a new tenancy of the whole of the property comprised in the relevant tenancy were granted to the tenant by order of the court and the duration of that new tenancy were the same as the duration of the new tenancy which is actually granted to the tenant.

(8) In this section and section 24D of this Act "the relevant tenancy" has the same meaning as in section 24A of this Act.

Amount of interim rent in any other case

24D—(1) The interim rent in a case where section 24C of this Act does not apply is the rent which it is reasonable for the tenant to pay while the relevant tenancy continues by virtue of section 24 of this Act.

(2) In determining the interim rent under subsection (1) above the court shall have regard—

(a) to the rent payable under the terms of the relevant tenancy; and

(b) to the rent payable under any sub-tenancy of part of the property comprised in the relevant tenancy,

but otherwise subsections (1) and (2) of section 34 of this Act shall apply to the determination as they would apply to the determination of a rent under that section if a new tenancy from year to year of the whole of the property comprised in the relevant tenancy were granted to the tenant by order of the court.

(3) If the court—

    (a) has made an order for the grant of a new tenancy and has ordered payment of interim rent in accordance with section 24C of this Act, but

    (b) either—

        (i) it subsequently revokes under section 36(2) of this Act the order for the grant of a new tenancy; or

        (ii) the landlord and tenant agree not to act on the order,

the court on the application of the landlord or the tenant shall determine a new interim rent in accordance with subsections (1) and (2) above without a further application under section 24A(1) of this Act.".

Compensation

Compensation for refusal of new tenancy

19.—(1) For section 37(1)(**a**) (compensation where new tenancy precluded on certain grounds) substitute—

"(1) Subject to the provisions of this Act, in a case specified in subsection (1A), (1B) or (1C) below (a "compensation case") the tenant shall be entitled on quitting the holding to recover from the landlord by way of compensation an amount determined in accordance with this section.

(1A) The first compensation case is where on the making of an application by the tenant under section 24(1) of this Act the court is precluded (whether by subsection (1) or subsection (2) of section 31 of this Act) from making an order for the grant of a new tenancy by reason of any of the grounds specified in paragraphs (e), (f) and (g) of section 30(1) of this Act (the "compensation grounds") and not of any grounds specified in any other paragraph of section 30(1).

(1B) The second compensation case is where on the making of an application under section 29(2) of this Act the court is precluded (whether by section 29(4)(a) or section 31(2) of this Act) from making an order for the grant of a new tenancy by reason of any of the compensation grounds and not of any other grounds specified in section 30(1) of this Act.

(1C) The third compensation case is where—

    (a) the landlord's notice under section 25 of this Act or, as the case may be, under section 26(6) of this Act, states his opposition to the grant of a new tenancy on any of the compensation grounds and not on any other grounds specified in section 30(1) of this Act; and

    (b) either—

        (i) no application is made by the tenant under section 24(1) of this Act or by the landlord under section 29(2) of this Act; or

        (ii) such an application is made but is subsequently withdrawn.".

(2) In section 37(2)(**b**)—

    (a) for the words "subsections (5A) to (5E) of this section the said amount" substitute "the following provisions of this section, compensation under this section"; and

    (b) in paragraph (a), after the word "satisfied" insert "in relation to the whole of the holding".

(3) After section 37(3) insert—

"(3A) If the conditions specified in subsection (3) above are satisfied in relation to part of the holding but not in relation to the other part, the amount of compensation shall be the aggregate of sums calculated separately as compensation in respect of each part, and accordingly, for the purpose of calculating compensation in respect of a part any reference in this section to the holding shall be construed as a reference to that part.

(**a**) Section 37(1) was amended by section 11 of the Law of Property Act 1969 (c. 59).

(**b**) Section 37(2) has been amended by section 149(6) of the Local Government and Housing Act 1989 (c. 42), article 2 of the Local Government Finance (Miscellaneous Amendments and Repeal) Order 1990 (S.I. 1990 no. 1285), and section 193 of the Local Government, Planning and Land Act 1980 (c. 65).

(3B) Where section 44(1A) of this Act applies, the compensation shall be determined separately for each part and compensation determined for any part shall be recoverable only from the person who is the owner of an interest in that part which fulfils the conditions specified in section 44(1) of this Act.".

(4) In section 37(4), for the words "the circumstances mentioned in subsection (1) of this section" substitute "a compensation case".

Compensation for misrepresentation

20. After section 37 insert—

"Compensation for possession obtained by misrepresentation

37A.—(1) Where the court—
- (a) makes an order for the termination of the current tenancy but does not make an order for the grant of a new tenancy, or
- (b) refuses an order for the grant of a new tenancy,

and it subsequently made to appear to the court that the order was obtained, or the court was induced to refuse the grant, by misrepresentation or the concealment of material facts, the court may order the landlord to pay to the tenant such sum as appears sufficient as compensation for damage or loss sustained by the tenant as the result of the order or refusal.

(2) Where—
- (a) the tenant has quit the holding—
  - (i) after making but withdrawing an application under section 24(1) of this Act; or
  - (ii) without making such an application; and
- (b) it is made to appear to the court that he did so by reason of misrepresentation or the concealment of material facts,

the court may order the landlord to pay to the tenant such sum as appears sufficient as compensation for damage or loss sustained by the tenant as the result of quitting the holding.".

Agreements to exclude security of tenure

Amendments to section 38

21.—(1) In section 38(1) (restrictions on agreements excluding provisions of Part 2)(a) for "subsection (4) of this section" substitute "section 38A of this Act".

(2) Omit section 38(4).

Agreements to exclude sections 24 to 28

22.—(1) After section 38 insert—

"Agreements to exclude provisions of Part 2

38A.—(1) The persons who will be the landlord and the tenant in relation to a tenancy to be granted for a term of years certain which will be a tenancy to which this Part of this Act applies may agree that the provisions of sections 24 to 28 of this Act shall be excluded in relation to that tenancy.

(2) The persons who are the landlord and the tenant in relation to a tenancy to which this Part of this Act applies may agree that the tenancy shall be surrendered on such date or in such circumstances as may be specified in the agreement and on such terms (if any) as may be so specified.

(a) The words in section 38(1) which are being substituted by this Order, together with section 38(4), were themselves added by section 5 of the Law of Property Act 1969.

(3) An agreement under subsection (1) above shall be void unless—

    (a) the landlord has served on the tenant a notice in the form, or substantially in the form, set out in Schedule 1 to the Regulatory Reform (Business Tenancies) (England and Wales) Order 2003 ("the 2003 Order"); and

    (b) the requirements specified in Schedule 2 to that Order are met.

(4) An agreement under subsection (2) above shall be void unless—

    (a) the landlord has served on the tenant a notice in the form, or substantially in the form, set out in Schedule 3 to the 2003 Order; and

    (b) the requirements specified in Schedule 4 to that Order are met."

(2) Schedules 1 to 4 to this Order shall have effect.

Duties to give information

Provision of information

23. For section 40 substitute—

"Duties of tenants and landlords of business premises to give information to each other

40.—(1) Where a person who is an owner of an interest in reversion expectant (whether immediately or not) on a tenancy of any business premises has served on the tenant a notice in the prescribed form requiring him to do so, it shall be the duty of the tenant to give the appropriate person in writing the information specified in subsection (2) below.

(2) That information is—

    (a) whether the tenant occupies the premises or any part of them wholly or partly for the purposes of a business carried on by him;

    (b) whether his tenancy has effect subject to any sub-tenancy on which his tenancy is immediately expectant and, if so—

        (i) what premises are comprised in the sub-tenancy;

        (ii) for what term it has effect (or, if it is terminable by notice, by what notice it can be terminated),

        (iii) what is the rent payable under it;

        (iv) who is the sub-tenant;

        (v) (to the best of his knowledge and belief) whether the sub-tenant is in occupation of the premises or of part of the premises comprised in the sub-tenancy and, if not, what is the sub-tenant's address;

        (vi) whether an agreement is in force excluding in relation to the sub-tenancy the provisions of sections 24 to 28 of this Act; and

        (vii) whether a notice has been given under section 25 or 26(6) of this Act, or a request has been made under section 26 of this Act, in relation to the sub-tenancy and, if so, details of the notice or request; and

    (c) (to the best of his knowledge and belief) the name and address of any other person who owns an interest in reversion in any part of the premises.

(3) Where the tenant of any business premises who is a tenant under such a tenancy as is mentioned in section 26(1) of this Act has served on a reversioner or a reversioner's mortgagee in possession a notice in the prescribed form requiring him to do so, it shall be the duty of the person on whom the notice is served to give the appropriate person in writing the information specified in subsection (4) below.

(4) That information is—

    (a) whether he is the owner of the fee simple in respect of the premises or any part of them or the mortgagee in possession of such an owner,

    (b) if he is not, then (to the best of his knowledge and belief)—

        (i) the name and address of the person who is his or, as the case may be, his mortgagor's immediate landlord in respect of those premises or of the part in respect of which he or his mortgagor is not the owner in fee simple;

10

    (ii) for what term his or his mortgagor's tenancy has effect and what is the earliest date (if any) at which that tenancy is terminable by notice to quit given by the landlord; and

    (iii) whether a notice has been given under section 25 or 26(6) of this Act, or a request has been made under section 26 of this Act, in relation to the tenancy and, if so, details of the notice or request;

  (c) (to the best of his knowledge and belief) the name and address of any other person who owns an interest in reversion in any part of the premises; and

  (d) if he is a reversioner, whether there is a mortgagee in possession of his interest in the premises and, if so, (to the best of his knowledge and belief) what is the name and address of the mortgagee.

(5) A duty imposed on a person by this section is a duty—

  (a) to give the information concerned within the period of one month beginning with the date of service of the notice; and

  (b) if within the period of six months beginning with the date of service of the notice that person becomes aware that any information which has been given in pursuance of the notice is not, or is no longer, correct, to give the appropriate person correct information within the period of one month beginning with the date on which he becomes aware.

(6) This section shall not apply to a notice served by or on the tenant more than two years before the date on which apart from this Act his tenancy would come to an end by effluxion of time or could be brought to an end by notice to quit given by the landlord.

(7) Except as provided by section 40A of this Act, the appropriate person for the purposes of this section and section 40A(1) of this Act is the person who served the notice under subsection (1) or (3) above.

(8) In this section—

"business premises" means premises used wholly or partly for the purposes of a business;

"mortgagee in possession" includes a receiver appointed by the mortgagee or by the court who is in receipt of the rents and profits, and "his mortgagor" shall be construed accordingly;

"reversioner" means any person having an interest in the premises, being an interest in reversion expectant (whether immediately or not) on the tenancy;

"reversioner's mortgagee in possession" means any person being a mortgagee in possession in respect of such an interest; and

"sub-tenant" includes a person retaining possession of any premises by virtue of the Rent (Agriculture) Act 1976 or the Rent Act 1977 after the coming to an end of a sub-tenancy, and "sub-tenancy" includes a right so to retain possession.".

Section 40 duties in transfer cases

24.   After section 40 insert the following sections—

"Duties in transfer cases

40A.—(1) If a person on whom a notice under section 40(1) or (3) of this Act has been served has transferred his interest in the premises or any part of them to some other person and gives the appropriate person notice in writing—

  (a) of the transfer of his interest; and

  (b) of the name and address of the person to whom he transferred it,

on giving the notice he ceases in relation to the premises or (as the case may be) to that part to be under any duty imposed by section 40 of this Act.

(2) If—

  (a) the person who served the notice under section 40(1) or (3) of this Act ("the transferor") has transferred his interest in the premises to some other person ("the transferee"); and

      (b) the transferor or the transferee has given the person required to give the information notice in writing—

          (i) of the transfer; and

          (ii) of the transferee's name and address,

the appropriate person for the purposes of section 40 of this Act and subsection (1) above is the transferee.

    (3) If—

      (a) a transfer such as is mentioned in paragraph (a) of subsection (2) above has taken place; but

      (b) neither the transferor nor the transferee has given a notice such as is mentioned in paragraph (b) of that subsection,

any duty imposed by section 40 of this Act may be performed by giving the information either to the transferor or to the transferee.

Proceedings for breach of duties to give information

    40B. A claim that a person has broken any duty imposed by section 40 of this Act may be made the subject of civil proceedings for breach of statutory duty; and in any such proceedings a court may order that person to comply with that duty and may make an award of damages.".

Miscellaneous amendments

Termination by tenant of tenancy

    25.—(1) After section 27(1) (termination by tenant of fixed term tenancy at end of term)(a) insert—

    "(1A) Section 24 of this Act shall not have effect in relation to a tenancy for a term of years certain where the tenant is not in occupation of the property comprised in the tenancy at the time when, apart from this Act, the tenancy would come to an end by effluxion of time.".

    (2) In section 27(2) (termination by tenant of fixed term tenancy continuing by virtue of section 24)—

      (a) after "of this Act" insert "shall not come to an end by reason only of the tenant ceasing to occupy the property comprised in the tenancy but"; and

      (b) omit the word "quarter".

    (3) After that subsection insert—

    "(3) Where a tenancy is terminated under subsection (2) above, any rent payable in respect of a period which begins before, and ends after, the tenancy is terminated shall be apportioned, and any rent paid by the tenant in excess of the amount apportioned to the period before termination shall be recoverable by him.".

Maximum duration of new tenancy

    26. In section 33 (duration of new tenancy) for the word "fourteen" substitute the word "fifteen".

Divided reversions

    27.—(1) In section 44(1)(b) (meaning of "landlord"), for "the next following subsection," substitute "subsections (1A) and (2) below,".

    (2) After section 44(1) insert—

    "(1A) The reference in subsection (1) above to a person who is the owner of an interest such as is mentioned in that subsection is to be construed, where different persons own such interests in different parts of the property, as a reference to all those persons collectively.".

(a) Section 27 was amended by section 4(2) of the Law of Property Act 1969 (c. 59).
(b) Section 44(1) was amended by section 14(1) of the Law of Property Act 1969 (c. 59).

(3) In section 35(1)(a) (other terms of new tenancy), after the word "thereunder)" insert ", including, where different persons own interests which fulfil the conditions specified in section 44(1) of this Act in different parts of it, terms as to the apportionment of the rent,".

Final provisions

Consequential amendments, repeals and subordinate provisions

28.—(1) Schedule 5 to this Order, which contains amendments consequential on the provisions of this Order, shall have effect.

(2) The enactments specified in Schedule 6 to this Order are repealed to the extent mentioned in the third column of that Schedule.

(3) Schedules 1 to 4 to this Order are designated as subordinate provisions for the purposes of section 4 of the Regulatory Reform Act 2001.

(4) A subordinate provisions order relating to the subordinate provisions designated by paragraph (3) above shall be subject to annulment in pursuance of a resolution of either House of Parliament.

(5) The power to make a subordinate provisions order relating to those provisions is to be exercisable in relation to Wales by the National Assembly for Wales concurrently with a Minister of the Crown.

(6) Paragraph (4) above does not apply to a subordinate provisions order made by the National Assembly for Wales.

(7) The notices and statutory declarations set out in Schedules 1 to 4 to this Order shall be treated for the purposes of section 26 of the Welsh Language Act 1993(b) (power to prescribe Welsh forms) as if they were specified by an Act of Parliament; and accordingly the power conferred by section 26(2) of that Act may be exercised in relation to those notices and declarations.

Transitional provisions

29.—(1) Where, before this Order came into force—

    (a) the landlord gave the tenant notice under section 25 of the Act; or

    (b) the tenant made a request for a new tenancy in accordance with section 26 of the Act,

nothing in this Order has effect in relation to the notice or request or anything done in consequence of it.

(2) Nothing in this Order has effect in relation—

    (a) to an agreement—

        (i) for the surrender of a tenancy which was made before this Order came into force and which fell within section 24(2)(b) of the Act; or

        (ii) which was authorised by the court under section 38(4) of the Act before this Order came into force; or

    (b) to a notice under section 27(2) of the Act which was given by the tenant to the immediate landlord before this Order came into force.

(3) Any provision in a tenancy which requires an order under section 38(4) of the Act to be obtained in respect of any subtenancy shall, so far as is necessary after the coming into force of this Order, be construed as if it required the procedure mentioned in section 38A of the Act to be followed, and any related requirement shall be construed accordingly.

(a) Section 35(1) was numbered as such by paragraph 4 of Schedule 1 to the Landlord and Tenant (Covenants) Act 1995 (c. 30).
(b) 1993 c. 38.

(4) If a person has, before the coming into force of this Order, entered into an agreement to take a tenancy, any provision in that agreement which requires an order under section 38(4) of the Act to be obtained in respect of the tenancy shall continue to be effective, notwithstanding the repeal of that provision by Article 21(2) of this Order, and the court shall retain jurisdiction to make such an order.

(5) Article 20 above does not have effect where the tenant quit the holding before this Order came into force.

(6) Nothing in Articles 23 and 24 above applies to a notice under section 40 of the Act served before this Order came into force.

Signed by authority of the First Secretary of State

Keith Hill
Minister of State
1st December 2003   Office of the Deputy Prime Minister

SCHEDULE 1

FORM OF NOTICE THAT SECTIONS 24 TO 28 OF THE LANDLORD AND TENANT ACT 1954 ARE NOT TO APPLY TO A BUSINESS TENANCY

To:

....

....

.... [*Name and address of tenant*]

From:

....

....

.... [*Name and address of landlord*]

IMPORTANT NOTICE

You are being offered a lease without security of tenure. Do not commit yourself to the lease unless you have read this message carefully and have discussed it with a professional adviser.

Business tenants normally have security of tenure – the right to stay in their business premises when the lease ends.

If you commit yourself to the lease you will be giving up these important legal rights.

- You will have **no right** to stay in the premises when the lease ends.

- Unless the landlord chooses to offer you another lease, you will need to leave the premises.

- You will be unable to claim compensation for the loss of your business premises, unless the lease specifically gives you this right.

- If the landlord offers you another lease, you will have no right to ask the court to fix the rent.

It is therefore important to get professional advice – from a qualified surveyor, lawyer or accountant - before agreeing to give up these rights.

If you receive this notice at least **14 days** before committing yourself to the lease, you will need to sign a simple declaration that you have received this notice and have accepted its consequences, before signing the lease.

But if you do not receive at least 14 days notice, you will need to sign a "statutory" declaration. To do so, you will need to visit an independent solicitor (or someone else empowered to administer oaths).

Unless there is a special reason for committing yourself to the lease sooner, you may want to ask the landlord to let you have at least 14 days to consider whether you wish to give up your statutory rights. If you then decided to go ahead with the agreement to exclude the protection of the Landlord and Tenant Act 1954, you would only need to make a simple declaration, and so you would not need to make a separate visit to an independent solicitor.

First port of call for purchasing property

The Euro 2004 football tournament will introduce many to Portugal for the first time, and new tax reforms have now made this an even more popular location for buying a home abroad. Vicky Rodrigues looks at how lawyers should advise interested clients

Portugal has long been a prime destination for foreign second home buyers – it is one of the strongest sectors of the Portuguese economy and a source of income for the Portuguese Inland Revenue.

For this reason, successive Portuguese governments have promised sweeping reforms in property taxation. The Portuguese administration finally put pen to paper and on 12 November 2003 Decree Law 287/2003 was published in Portugal's official *Gazette* – it was a declaration of war on tax evasion by Portuguese tax residents.

However, non-residents for tax purposes, who are not liable to declare to the Portuguese revenue their worldwide income, but only their Portuguese-source income, were also inevitably caught up in this legislation.

This law provides for a complete overhaul of all property taxes in Portugal with far-reaching effects for both existing and future property owners – residents and non-residents alike. The aim of the Portuguese authorities is to reduce rates of tax, make taxable values realistic and enforce anti-avoidance measures, ensuring that the burden of tax is distributed equitably.

The reform has two main lines of orientation:
- The need to revalue all properties and to ensure that the taxable value of properties (on which most property taxes are levied) equates as far as possible to their market value.
- A crackdown on the use of property owning offshore companies as a means of tax evasion.

The Portuguese government has targeted an important factor in property taxation – the taxable value of property, as most property taxes are based on this. Owing to the previous absence of

Net gains: tax burden in Portugal is almost halved

a framework under which these values could be updated, it was the new property owners who were charged a disproportional high tax in comparison with the old property owners.

The revaluing process has therefore begun. There are extensive criteria on which these valuations will be based, such as age of property, size, construction areas, location and the property's condition. And it will be on this new found (and considerably higher) taxable value that the scale of this tax reform will be felt.

Any property changing hands will automatically be revalued. However, interim measures have been approved (the government works on a five-year transitional period) and all property tax values have been updated in accordance with a table of coefficients published by the government.

In relation to municipal tax (IMI), the existing bands of 0.8 to 1.2% are to be restricted to 0.2 to 0.5% of the taxable value. Until revaluation occurs, a taxable rate of between 0.4% and 0.8% of the corrected tax value will be payable, with a yearly ceiling on increases until 2008. The rates for transfer tax (IMT, previously SISA) have also been lowered.

The second intention of this reform was to enact anti-avoidance legislation in respect of offshore companies, similar to what occurred in other European countries in the 1980s. If the advantage of buying a property using an offshore company was to avoid paying certain taxes – such as transfer tax, capital gains tax, notarial fees, registration fees, stamp duty and inheritance tax – the reform has done away with most of the incentives that first

attracted purchasers to offshore companies. While at the same time it has escalated the overhead on tax haven-based structures.

The treatment of offshore property owning companies whose registered office is in a tax haven (a list has been published by the Minister of Finance and has been added to in recent months) such as Gibraltar, Isle of Man and Channel Islands will be subject to draconian measures:
- 15% transfer tax on purchase;
- 25% corporation tax on gains when sold;
- 5% municipal tax per annum on corrected taxable value/revaluation;
- Corporation tax on 1/15 of the patrimonial value of the property.

In addition, these companies do not qualify for tax benefits or exemptions and the transitional provisions do not apply.

The reforms mean that many homeowners are now faced with a pending need to seek a viable solution for the restructuring of their ownership. The problem is complex and dependent on many variables.

However, it may be more costly passively to let events unfold. The easiest and most straightforward option is no doubt to transfer the property into one's own name. But, in some cases this will be an expensive option, not only because of the costs with the transfer, but also in terms of capital gains tax. Property in Portugal has rocketed, but this rise in prices has come as a mixed blessing in terms of capital gains tax. To make matters worse, the gain is only on paper, while the tax must be paid in hard cash.

Another option is redomiciling

the company to another, non-black-listed jurisdiction. However, it is important to note that this may be a temporary measure as not only may the Portuguese tax authorities consider that it is a form of escaping compliance, but the black-list is updated constantly.

One can also bring one's company onshore to Portugal, if the country of origin allows it. The company will then become, to all intents and purposes, Portuguese. This is a relatively straightforward procedure, and as there is no transfer of ownership, any capital gains are not crystallized (although it is important to note that the original acquisition value remains for the purposes of calculating capital gains on a future sale). The company will be liable to Portuguese corporation tax and will need to make annual returns.

Another option involves the offshore company being wound up in its country of origin and its asset (namely, the property in Portugal) being distributed to its shareholders. This is then registered in Portugal to reflect the change in ownership. The appropriateness of this solution depends on the tax residence of the shareholders.

It is true that there are many 'victims' of this legislation. For example, there have been foreign buyers who had no knowledge of or understanding of the nature of offshore companies until they purchased properties in Portugal. They now face tax liabilities that they are unable to meet. There have also been examples of pensioners on relatively low incomes who have been age-barred from obtaining loans. But one can only salute the spirit behind these reforms, which is to combat massive tax evasion in the property industry and bring more equality to the system.

For new property owners, the tax reforms can only be good news – in many cases, the tax burden on buying property in Portugal is almost halved. For existing property owners, it is time to take stock and tax planning advice and seek the best solution for individual cases.
Vicky Rodrigues of Lisbon-based Neville de Rougemont & Associados is a Portuguese advogada and an English solicitor

Why landlords must proceed with care

Recent reforms to part II of the Landlord and Tenant Act 1954 change the rules governing how a tenancy is excluded from the protection of the legislation. Therefore, it is important that landlords ensure procedure is satisfied before any agreement for lease is entered into, says Jason Hunter

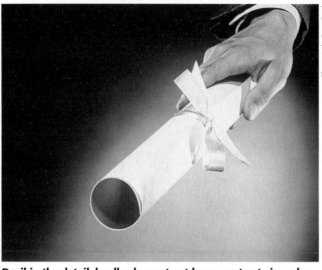

Devil in the detail: landlords must get lease contracts in order

As all landlord and tenant lawyers should now know, changes to part II of the Landlord and Tenant Act 1954 were introduced on 1 June. The reforms are contained in the Regulatory Reform (Business Tenancies) (England and Wales) Order 2003 — SI 2003 No. 3096 (RRO).

The Act, its procedures and time limits, have caused many problems in the past; notwithstanding the changes, there is still scope for negligence.

Perhaps the most significant change introduced by the order is the procedure for contracting out. Under the law and procedure — which was current until 31 May — for a tenancy to be excluded from the protection of the Act, the parties must jointly apply to court for an order under section 38(4).

From 1 June, the court-based scheme ceased to apply (except in relation to pre-existing agreements to seek such an order). From now on, the protection of the Act can be excluded by a notice and declaration procedure, summarised as follows:

● Before the proposed tenancy is entered into or the parties become contractually bound to do so, the landlord must give to the tenant a notice in the form set out in schedule 1 to the order.

● If the notice is given 14 days or more before the proposed tenancy is entered into or the parties become contractually bound to do so, the tenant (or someone duly authorised to do so on his behalf) must make a simple declaration in the form set out in paragraph 7 of schedule 2 to the order.

● If the schedule 1 notice is given less than 14 days before the proposed tenancy is entered into or the parties become contractually bound to enter into a tenancy, the tenant (or someone duly authorised to do so on his behalf) must make a statutory declaration in the form set out in paragraph 8 of schedule 2 to the order.

● In either case, a reference to the notice, the requisite declaration and the agreement under new section 38A(1) of the Act must be contained in or endorsed on the instrument creating the tenancy.

If any of these requirements are not met, the tenancy may not be excluded from the protection of the Act. Therefore, it is a matter of concern to the landlord and any advisers to ensure that the procedure is satisfied.

Under the old regime, parties would often enter into an agreement for lease conditional on then obtaining the necessary court order. It would seem that, by the use of the words 'becomes contractually bound to [enter into a tenancy]', such an arrangement will no longer work and the new procedure should be followed before any agreement for lease is entered into (although it may be conditional for other reasons).

The position in relation to agreements to surrender tenancies that are already protected by the Act are similar and set out in schedules 3 and 4 to the order.

An important requirement of the Act is that a protected tenancy can only be brought to an end (otherwise than by, say, forfeiture) by operating the procedures for termination contained in sections 25 and 26. New provisions apply where a section 25 notice or section 26 request is given on or after 1 June 2004 and what follows in this section only applies in those circumstances. If a notice or request has been given before then, the old procedure will continue to apply.

There are two new section 25 notices — one where the landlord does not object to the tenant having a new tenancy and another where it does — and a new section 26 request (see schedule 2 to the Landlord and Tenant Act 1954, Part 2 (Notices) Regulations 2004 — SI 2004 No. 1005)

Under the pre-1 June procedure, a tenant was obliged to give a counternotice in response to a landlord's section 25 notice. Under the procedure introduced on 1 June, a tenant does not have to do so.

The landlord had to give a counternotice to a tenant's section 26 request (but only if the landlord wished to object to the tenant having a new tenancy on one of the grounds in section 30(1)). Now the landlord still needs to do so.

Formerly, only the tenant could apply to court not less than two months or later than four months from the giving of the section 25 notice or section 26 request. Failure to do so resulted in the loss of an entitlement to seek a new tenancy.

Since 1 June, either the landlord or the tenant may apply for a tenancy. As before, the failure to apply to court (whoever does it) will result in the loss by the tenant of an entitlement to seek a tenancy. Furthermore, the landlord may apply for the termination of the tenancy where it has objected on one of the statutory grounds.

A permitted application must be made before the end of the 'statutory period', which is the date specified in the section 25 notice or the day before the date specified in the section 26. That period can be extended by written agreement entered into before the end of the statutory period. There can be further similar extension agreements.

In addition, applications for interim rent will be capable of being made by either the landlord or the tenant. There are some complex provisions concerning the date from which interim rent is to be paid and the amount it will be (see sections 24A, 24B, 24C and 24D).

With the changes to the Act by the order, the part 56 Civil Procedure rules require modification. They will only apply where the new regime applies, namely where a section 25 notice or section 26 request is given on or after 1 June 2004.

So, there will be two types of procedure running in tandem for what may be some years. Possibly the most important of the changes to the new procedure is that the automatic three-month stay of proceedings that, under the old system, could be obtained by a landlord, will no longer be available.

The changed rules also deal with the possibility of a multiplicity of proceedings since it is possible that both the landlord and tenant could issue proceedings.

Jason Hunter is the head of contentious property at London-based law firm Russell-Cooke and chairman of the Property Litigation Association. He is the author of Business Tenancies: A Guide to the New Law, *published by Law Society Publishing in June. The book provides practical guidance on the recent changes to part II of the Landlord and Tenant Act 1954 and can be ordered direct from Marston Book Services, tel: 01235 465 656*

REQUIREMENTS FOR A VALID AGREEMENT THAT SECTIONS 24 TO 28 OF THE LANDLORD AND TENANT ACT 1954 ARE NOT TO APPLY TO A BUSINESS TENANCY

1.   The following are the requirements referred to in section 38A(3)(b) of the Act.

2.   Subject to paragraph 4, the notice referred to in section 38A(3)(a) of the Act must be served on the tenant not less than 14 days before the tenant enters into the tenancy to which it applies, or (if earlier) becomes contractually bound to do so.

3.   If the requirement in paragraph 2 is met, the tenant, or a person duly authorised by him to do so, must, before the tenant enters into the tenancy to which the notice applies, or (if earlier) becomes contractually bound to do so, make a declaration in the form, or substantially in the form, set out in paragraph 7.

4.   If the requirement in paragraph 2 is not met, the notice referred to in section 38A(3)(a) of the Act must be served on the tenant before the tenant enters into the tenancy to which it applies, or (if earlier) becomes contactually bound to do so, and the tenant, or a person duly authorised by him to do so, must before that time make a statutory declaration in the form, or substantially in the form, set out in paragraph 8.

5.   A reference to the notice and, where paragraph 3 applies, the declaration or, where paragraph 4 applies, the statutory declaration must be contained in or endorsed on the instrument creating the tenancy.

6.   The agreement under section 38A(1) of the Act, or a reference to the agreement, must be contained in or endorsed upon the instrument creating the tenancy.

7.   The form of declaration referred to in paragraph 3 is as follows:—

I   ....(*name of declarant*) of.......................................(*address*) declare that—

1.   I/.................................(*name of tenant*) propose(s) to enter into a tenancy of premises at.......................................(*address of premises*) for a term commencing on ....

2.   I/The tenant propose(s) to enter into an agreement with... (*name of landlord*) that the provisions of sections 24 to 28 of the Landlord and Tenant Act 1954 (security of tenure) shall be excluded in relation to the tenancy.

3.   The landlord has, not less than 14 days before I/the tenant enter(s) into the tenancy, or (if earlier) become(s) contractually bound to do so served on me/the tenant a notice in the form, or substantially in the form, set out in Schedule 1 to the Regulatory Reform (Business Tenancies) (England and Wales) Order 2003. The form of notice set out in that Schedule is reproduced below.

4.   I have/The tenant has read the notice referred to in paragraph 3 above and accept(s) the consequences of entering into the agreement referred to in paragraph 2 above.

5.   (*as appropriate*) I am duly authorised by the tenant to make this declaration.

DECLARED this..day of...

To:

....

....

.... [*Name and address of tenant*]

From:

....

....

.... [*name and address of landlord*]

You are being offered a lease without security of tenure. Do not commit yourself to the lease unless you have read this message carefully and have discussed it with a professional adviser.

Business tenants normally have security of tenure – the right to stay in their business premises when the lease ends.

If you commit yourself to the lease you will be giving up these important legal rights.

- You will have **no right** to stay in the premises when the lease ends.

- Unless the landlord chooses to offer you another lease, you will need to leave the premises.

- You will be unable to claim compensation for the loss of your business premises, unless the lease specifically gives you this right.

- If the landlord offers you another lease, you will have no right to ask the court to fix the rent.

It is therefore important to get professional advice – from a qualified surveyor, lawyer or accountant – before agreeing to give up these rights.

If you want to ensure that you can stay in the same business premises when the lease ends, you should consult your adviser about another form of lease that does not exclude the protection of the Landlord and Tenant Act 1954.

If you receive this notice at least 14 days before committing yourself to the lease, you will need to sign a simple declaration that you have received this notice and have accepted its consequences, before signing the lease.

But if you do not receive at least 14 days notice, you will need to sign a "statutory" declaration.   To do so, you will need to visit an independent solicitor (or someone else empowered to administer oaths).

Unless there is a special reason for committing yourself to the lease sooner, you may want to ask the landlord to let you have at least 14 days to consider whether you wish to give up your statutory rights. If you then decided to go ahead with the agreement to exclude the protection of the Landlord and Tenant Act 1954, you would only need to make a simple declaration, and so you would not need to make a separate visit to an independent solicitor.

8. The form of statutory declaration referred to in paragraph 4 is as follows:—

I..(*name of declarant*) of ....(*address*) do solemnly and sincerely declare that—

1. I ....(*name of tenant*) propose(s) to enter into a tenancy of premises at.......................................(*address of premises*) for a term commencing on...

2. I/The tenant propose(s) to enter into an agreement with.. (name of landlord) that the provisions of sections 24 to 28 of the Landlord and Tenant Act 1954 (security of tenure) shall be excluded in relation to the tenancy.

3. The landlord has served on me/the tenant a notice in the form, or substantially in the form, set out in Schedule 1 to the Regulatory Reform (Business Tenancies) (England and Wales) Order 2003. The form of notice set out in that Schedule is reproduced below.

4. I have/The tenant has read the notice referred to in paragraph 3 above and accept(s) the consequences of entering into the agreement referred to in paragraph 2 above.

5. (*as appropriate*) I am duly authorised by the tenant to make this declaration.

To:

....

....

.... [*name and address of tenant*]

From:

....

....

.... [*Name and address of landlord*]

You are being offered a lease without security of tenure. Do not commit yourself to the lease unless you have read this message carefully and have discussed it with a professional adviser.

Business tenants normally have security of tenure – the right to stay in their business premises when the lease ends.

If you commit yourself to the lease you will be giving up these important legal rights.

- You will have **no right** to stay in the premises when the lease ends.

- Unless the landlord chooses to offer you another lease, you will need to leave the premises.

- You will be unable to claim compensation for the loss of your business premises, unless the lease specifically gives you this right.

- If the landlord offers you another lease, you will have no right to ask the court to fix the rent.

It is therefore important to get professional advice – from a qualified surveyor, lawyer or accountant – before agreeing to give up these rights.

If you want to ensure that you can stay in the same business premises when the lease ends, you should consult your adviser about another form of lease that does not exclude the protection of the Landlord and Tenant Act 1954.

If you receive this notice at least 14 days before committing yourself to the lease, you will need to sign a simple declaration that you have received this notice and have accepted its consequences, before signing the lease.

But if you do not receive at least 14 days notice, you will need to sign a "statutory" declaration.   To do so, you will need to visit an independent solicitor (or someone else empowered to administer oaths).

Unless there is a special reason for committing yourself to the lease sooner, you may want to ask the landlord to let you have at least 14 days to consider whether you wish to give up your statutory rights. If you then decided to go ahead with the agreement to exclude the protection of the Landlord and Tenant Act 1954, you would only need to make a simple declaration, and so you would not need to make a separate visit to an independent solicitor.

AND I make this solemn declaration conscientiously believing the same to be true and by virtue of the Statutory Declaration Act 1835.

DECLARED at .... this .... day of......................................

Before me

(*signature of person before whom declaration is made*)

A commissioner for oaths *or* A solicitor empowered to administer oaths or (*as appropriate*)

SCHEDULE 3

Article 22(2)

FORM OF NOTICE THAT AN AGREEMENT TO SURRENDER A BUSINESS TENANCY IS TO BE MADE

To:

....

....

.... [*name and address of tenant*]

From:

....

....

.... [*Name and address of landlord*]

Do not commit yourself to any agreement to surrender your lease unless you have read this message carefully and discussed it with a professional adviser.

Normally, you have the right to renew your lease when it expires. By committing yourself to an agreement to surrender, **you will be giving up this important statutory right**.

- You will **not** be able to continue occupying the premises beyond the date provided for under the agreement for surrender, **unless** the landlord chooses to offer you a further term (in which case you would lose the right to ask the court to determine the new rent). You will need to leave the premises.

- You will be unable to claim compensation for the loss of your premises, unless the lease or agreement for surrender gives you this right.

A qualified surveyor, lawyer or accountant would be able to offer you professional advice on your options.

You do not have to commit yourself to the agreement to surrender your lease unless you want to.

If you receive this notice at least 14 days before committing yourself to the agreement to surrender, you will need to sign a simple declaration that you have received this notice and have accepted its consequences, before signing the agreement to surrender.

But if you do not receive at least 14 days notice, you will need to sign a "statutory" declaration. To do so, you will need to visit an independent solicitor (or someone else empowered to administer oaths).

Unless there is a special reason for committing yourself to the agreement to surrender sooner, you may want to ask the landlord to let you have at least 14 days to consider whether you wish to give up your statutory rights. If you then decided to go ahead with the agreement to end your lease, you would only need to make a simple declaration, and so you would not need to make a separate visit to an independent solicitor.

SCHEDULE 4

REQUIREMENTS FOR A VALID AGREEMENT TO SURRENDER A BUSINESS TENANCY

1.   The following are the requirements referred to in section 38A(4)(b) of the Act.

2.   Subject to paragraph 4, the notice referred to in section 38A(4)(a) of the Act must be served on the tenant not less than 14 days before the tenant enters into the agreement under section 38A(2) of the Act, or (if earlier) becomes contractually bound to do so.

3.   If the requirement in paragraph 2 is met, the tenant or a person duly authorised by him to do so, must, before the tenant enters into the agreement under section 38A(2) of the Act, or (if earlier) becomes contractually bound to do so, make a declaration in the form, or substantially in the form, set out in paragraph 6.

4.   If the requirement in paragraph 2 is not met, the notice referred to in section 38A(4)(a) of the Act must be served on the tenant before the tenant enters into the agreement under section 38A(2) of the Act, or (if earlier) becomes contractually bound to do so, and the tenant, or a person duly authorised by him to do so, must before that time make a statutory declaration in the form, or substantially in the form, set out in paragraph 7.

5.   A reference to the notice and, where paragraph 3 applies, the declaration or, where paragraph 4 applies, the statutory declaration must be contained in or endorsed on the instrument creating the agreement under section 38A(2).

6.   The form of declaration referred to in paragraph 3 is as follows:—

I ....(*name of declarant*) of ....(*address*) declare that—

1.   I have/ .... (*name of tenant*) has a tenancy of premises at .... (*address of premises*) for a term commencing on ....

2.   I/The tenant propose(s) to enter into an agreement with... (*name of landlord*) to surrender the tenancy on a date or in circumstances specified in the agreement.

3.   The landlord has not less than 14 days before I/the tenant enter(s) into the agreement referred to in paragraph 2 above, or (if earlier) become(s) contractually bound to do so, served on me/the tenant a notice in the form, or substantially in the form, set out in Schedule 3 to Regulatory Reform (Business Tenancies) (England and Wales) Order 2003. The form of notice set out in that Schedule is reproduced below.

4.   I have/the tenant has read the notice referred to in paragraph 3 above and accept(s) the consequences of entering into the agreement referred to in paragraph 2 above.

5.   (*as appropriate*) I am duly authorised by the tenant to make this declaration.

DECLARED this..day of..

To:

....
....
.... [*name and address of tenant*]

From:

....
....
.... [*Name and address of landlord*]

7. The form of statutory declaration referred to in paragraph 4 is as follows:—

I ....(*name of declarant*) of ....(*address*) do solemnly and sincerely declare that—

1. I have/.. (*name of tenant*) has a tenancy of premises at .... (*address of premises*) for a term commencing on ....

2. I/The tenant propose(s) to enter into an agreement with.. (*name of landlord*) to surrender the tenancy on a date or in circumstances specified in the agreement.

3. The landlord has served on me/the tenant a notice in the form, or substantially in the form, set out in Schedule 3 to the Regulatory Reform (Business Tenancies) (England and Wales) Order 2003. The form of notice set out in that Schedule is reproduced below.

4. I have/The tenant has read the notice referred to in paragraph 3 above and accept(s) the consequences of entering into the agreement referred to in paragraph 2 above.

5. (*as appropriate*) I am duly authorised by the tenant to make this declaration.

To:

....
....
.... *[name and address of tenant]*

From:

....
....
.... *[Name and address of landlord]*

IMPORTANT NOTICE FOR TENANT

<u>Do not commit yourself to any agreement to surrender your lease unless you have read this message carefully and discussed it with a professional adviser.</u>

Normally, you have the right to renew your lease when it expires. By committing yourself to an agreement to surrender, **<u>you will be giving up this important statutory right</u>**.

- You will **not** be able to continue occupying the premises beyond the date provided for under the agreement for surrender, **unless** the landlord chooses to offer you a further term (in which case you would lose the right to ask the court to determine the new rent). You will need to leave the premises.

- You will be unable to claim compensation for the loss of your premises, unless the lease or agreement for surrender gives you this right.

A qualified surveyor, lawyer or accountant would be able to offer you professional advice on your options.

<u>You do not have to commit yourself to the agreement to surrender your lease unless you want to.</u>

If you receive this notice at least 14 days before committing yourself to the agreement to surrender, you will need to sign a simple declaration that you have received this notice and have accepted its consequences, before signing the agreement to surrender.

<u>But if you do not receive at least 14 days notice, you will need to sign a "statutory" declaration.   To do so, you will need to visit an independent solicitor (or someone else empowered to administer oaths).</u>

Unless there is a special reason for committing yourself to the agreement to surrender sooner, you may want to ask the landlord to let you have at least 14 days to consider whether you wish to give up your statutory rights. If you then decided to go ahead with the agreement to end your lease, you would only need to make a simple declaration, and so you would not need to make a separate visit to an independent solicitor.

AND I make this solemn declaration conscientiously believing the same to be true and by virtue of the Statutory Declarations Act 1835

DECLARED at .... this .... day of......................................

Before me (*signature of person before whom declaration is made*)

A commissioner for oaths *or* A solicitor empowered to administer oaths *or* (*as appropriate*)

CONSEQUENTIAL AMENDMENTS

Landlord and Tenant Act 1954

1. The Act shall be amended as follows.

2. After section 14 insert—

"*Compensation for possession obtained by misrepresentation*

14A. Where an order is made for possession of the property comprised in a tenancy to which section 1 of this Act applies and it is subsequently made to appear to the court that the order was obtained by misrepresentation or the concealment of material facts, the court may order the landlord to pay to the tenant such a sum as appears sufficient as compensation for damage or loss sustained by the tenant as the result of the order.".

3. In section 26(1), for the words "tenancy under which he holds for the time being (hereinafter referred to as "the current tenancy")" substitute "current tenancy".

4. In section 38(2) and (3) for the words "the last foregoing section" substitute the words "section 37 of this Act".

5. In section 41A(6) for the words from "section 29(1)" to "jointly" substitute "section 29 of this Act for the grant of a new tenancy it may order the grant to be made to the business tenants or to them jointly".

6. In section 46—

(a) for the definition of "current tenancy" substitute—

""current tenancy" means the tenancy under which the tenant holds for the time being;"; and

(b) after the definition of "the holding" insert—

""interim rent" has the meaning given by section 24A(1) of this Act;";.

7. In sections 57(3)(a) and 58(1)(a)—

for the words "subsection (5) and" substitute the word "subsection"; and

after the word "under", in the second place where it occurs, insert the words "subsection (1) of".

8. In section 59(1), after "(3)" insert the words "to (3B)".

9. In section 64(1)(b), for the words "the said part II" substitute the words "under section 24(1) or 29(2) of this Act".

Leasehold Reform Act 1967

10. Schedule 3 to the Leasehold Reform Act 1967 (**a**) shall be amended as follows.

11. For paragraph 2(1) substitute—

"(1) Sub-paragraphs (1A) to (1E) below apply where a landlord's notice terminating the tenancy of any property has been given under section 4 or 25 of the Landlord and Tenant Act 1954 or served under paragraph 4(1) of Schedule 10 to the Local Government and Housing Act 1989 (whether or not that notice has effect to terminate the tenancy).

(1A) A claim to acquire the freehold or an extended lease of the property shall be of no effect if made after the relevant time, but this sub-paragraph is subject to sub-paragraphs (1D) and (1E) below.

(1B) In this paragraph (but subject to sub-paragraph (1C) below) "the relevant time" is the end of the period of two months beginning with the date on which the landlord's notice terminating the tenancy has been given or served.

(1C) Where—

(a) a landlord's notice terminating the tenancy has been given under section 25 of the Landlord and Tenant Act 1954, and

(b) the tenant applies to the court under section 24(1) of that Act for an order for the grant of a new tenancy before the end of the period of two months mentioned in sub-paragraph (1B) above,

"the relevant time" is the time when the application is made.

(1D) Sub-paragraph (1A) above shall not apply where the landlord gives his written consent to the claim being made after the relevant time.

(**a**) 1967 c. 88.

(1E) Where a tenant, having given notice of a desire to have the freehold, gives after the relevant time a further notice under section 9(3) of this Act of his inability or unwillingness to acquire the house and premises at the price he must pay, he may with the notice under section 9(3) give a notice of his desire to have an extended lease (if he then has a right to such a lease).".

12. After paragraph 2 insert—

"2A—(1) If—

    (a) the landlord commences proceedings under Part 2 of the Landlord and Tenant Act 1954; and

    (b) the tenant subsequently makes a claim to acquire the freehold or an extended lease of the property; and

    (c) paragraph 2 above does not render the claim of no effect,

no further steps shall be taken in the proceedings under Part 2 otherwise than for their dismissal and for the making of any consequential order.

(2) Section 64 of the Landlord and Tenant Act 1954 shall have no effect in a case to which sub-paragraph (1) above applies.".

13. After paragraph 10(2) insert—

"(2A) If the landlord's notice is under section 25 of the Landlord and Tenant Act 1954, sub-paragraph (2) above shall effect in relation to it as if in paragraph (b), after the word "operate" there were inserted the words "and no further proceedings may be taken by him under Part 2 of the Landlord and Tenant Act 1954.".

SCHEDULE 6

Article 28(2)

ENACTMENTS REPEALED

Chapter	Short title	Extent of repeal
2 and 3 Eliz. 2 c. 56	Landlord and Tenant Act 1954	Section 24(2)(b) and the word "or" immediately preceding it. Section 25(5). In section 27(2), the word "quarter". Section 30(3). Section 38(4). In section 42(1), the second paragraph. Section 55. In section 67, the words "(2) or".
1967 c. 88	Leasehold Reform Act 1967	In Schedule 3, paragraph 2(4)(b) and the word "and" immediately preceding it.
1969 c. 59	Law of Property Act 1969	Section 6.
1989 c. 40	Companies Act 1989	In Schedule 18, paragraph 3.

EXPLANATORY NOTE

(This note is not part of the Order)

This Order amends Part 2 of the Landlord and Tenant Act 1954 (security of tenure for business, professional and other non-residential tenants) ("Part 2"). Amongst other things, the Act provides that a tenancy to which Part 2 applies continues unless terminated in accordance with the provisions of the Act, and enables the tenant to apply to the court for a new tenancy.

Pending agreement on the terms of the new tenancy, the landlord may apply to the court for an interim rent. Where the parties fail to agree, the court fixes the terms of the new tenancy. The landlord may oppose renewal on specific grounds, certain of which give the tenant the right to claim compensation.

Before entering into a tenancy, the parties may apply jointly to the court for its approval to an agreement to exclude the provisions of Part 2 which confer security of tenure. Where the court has authorised such an agreement, the tenant has no right to renew the tenancy, and no statutory entitlement to compensation.

This Order implements most of the recommendations of the Law Commission contained in their 1992 paper *Business Tenancies: A Periodic Review of the Landlord and Tenant Act Part II* (Law Com No. 208). (Copies may be obtained from HMSO). A consultation paper *"Business tenancies legislation in England and Wales: the Government's proposals for reform"* was published by the Department of the Environment, Transport and the Regions in March 2001. Copies may be obtained from the Land and Property Division, Office of the Deputy Prime Minister, Eland House, Bressenden Place, London SW1E 5DU (tel: 020 7944 5559).

The main changes made by this Order are as follows:—

Renewal and termination procedures

Articles 3 to 9 change the procedures to be followed in order to renew a tenancy or to terminate it without renewal. Both landlords and tenants are permitted to apply to the court for the terms of a new tenancy to be settled. Landlords are permitted to apply for an order that the tenancy be terminated without renewal if they can make out one of the statutory grounds for opposition. The requirement for a tenant to serve a counternotice to a landlord's notice of termination is abolished.

Time limits for court applications

Articles 10 to 12 substitute new time limits for applications to the court to renew tenancies and enable the parties to agree to extend these.

Ownership and control of businesses

Articles 13 to 17 widen the circumstances in which landlord and tenant can operate the statutory procedures of Part 2. They provide, in particular, that an individual and any company he controls should be treated as one and the same for the purposes of those procedures and that companies controlled by one individual should be treated as members of a group of companies.

Interim rent

Article 18 introduces several changes relating to interim rent (rent payable pending renewal of a tenancy). Tenants as well as landlords are enabled to apply to the court for interim rent. The date from which any interim rent determined by the court is payable becomes the earliest date for renewal of the tenancy which could have been specified in the statutory notice served by the landlord or tenant. A new method for the calculation of the amount of interim rent is introduced where the landlord does not oppose renewal. The interim rent is set at the same level as the rent for the new tenancy (i.e. usually, the open market rent), but subject to adjustment where market conditions or the occupational terms of the tenancy change significantly during the interim period. In other circumstances, the rules for calculation of interim rent formerly in section 24A(3), and now contained in section 24D(2), continue to apply.

Compensation provisions

Articles 19 and 20 amend the rules relating to the compensation that a tenant may claim where his tenancy is not renewed. They amend the method of calculation of compensation where the tenant has occupied different parts of premises for different periods of time, and where different landlords control different parts. They also enable a tenant to claim compensation if he is induced not to apply to court, or to withdraw an application for renewal, because of a misrepresentation.

Contracting out and agreements to surrender

Articles 21 and 22 replace the requirement for both parties to apply to court for approval to an agreement to exclude security of tenure or to surrender a tenancy. The new procedure requires a landlord to serve a prescribed notice on the tenant at least 14 days before the parties enter into such an agreement. The tenant must sign a simple declaration that he has received and accepted the consequences of the notice. If the parties wish to waive the 14 day period, the tenant will have to sign a statutory declaration, rather than a simple declaration, that he has received and accepted the consequences of the notice. In the case of an agreement to exclude security of tenure, the declaration must be made before the tenant enters into the tenancy or becomes contractually bound to do so. In the case of an agreement to surrender, the declaration must be made before entering into the agreement. The forms of the notice, the simple declaration and the statutory declaration are set out in Schedules 1 to 4 to this Order.

Notices requiring information

Articles 23 and 24 increase the categories of information which a landlord and tenant can require the other to provide towards the end of a tenancy term, in order to enable effective use of the statutory renewal or termination process. They also impose an obligation to keep such information up to date for six months, make provision for parties which transfer their interests and clarify the powers of the court where a party fails to comply with obligations to provide or update information.

Tenants' notices of termination

Article 25 clarifies what a tenant must do to terminate a tenancy to which Part 2 applies. If a tenant has ceased to occupy the business premises at the expiry of the contractual term, no continuation tenancy arises. Where a tenancy has continued beyond the end of the fixed contractual term, the tenant must give three months notice, ending on any day. Where necessary, rent is apportioned.

Other

Article 26 increases the length of the term of a new tenancy that the court may order from 14 to 15 years. Article 27 makes provision for landlords of parts of the same business premises to make joint use of the Part 2 procedures.

Article 28 introduces Schedules 5 and 6 which make consequential amendments and repeals. Schedules 1 to 4, containing the form of the notices and declarations required by the new section 38A, which is inserted by article 22, are designated as subordinate provisions for the purposes of section 4 of the Regulatory Reform Act 2001. The National Assembly for Wales is given power concurrently with the Secretary of State to amend these provisions.

S T A T U T O R Y   I N S T R U M E N T S

2003 No. 3096

LANDLORD AND TENANT, ENGLAND AND WALES
REGULATORY REFORM

The Regulatory Reform (Business Tenancies) (England and Wales) Order 2003

Printed and published in the UK by The Stationery Office Limited
under the authority and superintendence of Carol Tullo, Controller of
Her Majesty's Stationery Office and Queen's Printer of Acts of Parliament.
E1541   11/2003   131541   19585

Published by TSO (The Stationery Office)
and available from:

TSO
(Mail, telephone and fax orders only)
PO Box 29, Norwich NR3 1GN
Telephone orders / enquiries 0870 600 5522
Fax orders 0870 600 5533
Email book.orders@tso.co.uk
Internet http://www.tso.co.uk/bookshop

TSO Shops
123 Kingsway, London WC2B 6PQ
020 7242 6393 Fax 020 7242 6394
68–69 Bull Street, Birmingham B4 6AD
0121 236 9696 Fax 0121 236 9699
9–21 Princess Street, Manchester M60 8AS
0161 834 7201 Fax 0161 833 0634
16 Arthur Street, Belfast BT1 4GD
028 9023 8451 Fax 028 9023 5401
18–19 High Street, Cardiff CF1 2BZ
029 2039 5548 Fax 029 2038 4347
71 Lothian Road, Edinburgh EH3 9AZ
0870 606 5566 Fax 0870 606 5588

Accredited Agents
(see Yellow Pages)

and through good booksellers

ISBN 0-11-048240-9

9 780110 482408